A

WEBSITE NAME:

WEBSITE ADDRESS:

USERNAME:

PASSWORD:

NOTES (EMAIL USED, ETC):

WEBSITE NAME:

WEBSITE ADDRESS:

USERNAME:

PASSWORD:

NOTES (EMAIL USED, ETC):

WEBSITE NAME:

WEBSITE ADDRESS:

USERNAME:

PASSWORD:

NOTES (EMAIL USED, ETC):

A

WEBSITE NAME:

WEBSITE ADDRESS:

USERNAME:

PASSWORD:

NOTES (EMAIL USED, ETC):

WEBSITE NAME:

WEBSITE ADDRESS:

USERNAME:

PASSWORD:

NOTES (EMAIL USED, ETC):

WEBSITE NAME:

WEBSITE ADDRESS:

USERNAME:

PASSWORD:

NOTES (EMAIL USED, ETC):

A

WEBSITE NAME:

WEBSITE ADDRESS:

USERNAME:

PASSWORD:

NOTES (EMAIL USED, ETC):

WEBSITE NAME:

WEBSITE ADDRESS:

USERNAME:

PASSWORD:

NOTES (EMAIL USED, ETC):

WEBSITE NAME:

WEBSITE ADDRESS:

USERNAME:

PASSWORD:

NOTES (EMAIL USED, ETC):

A

WEBSITE NAME:

WEBSITE ADDRESS:

USERNAME:

PASSWORD:

NOTES (EMAIL USED, ETC):

WEBSITE NAME:

WEBSITE ADDRESS:

USERNAME:

PASSWORD:

NOTES (EMAIL USED, ETC):

WEBSITE NAME:

WEBSITE ADDRESS:

USERNAME:

PASSWORD:

NOTES (EMAIL USED, ETC):

WEBSITE NAME:

B

WEBSITE ADDRESS:

USERNAME:

PASSWORD:

NOTES (EMAIL USED, ETC):

WEBSITE NAME:

WEBSITE ADDRESS:

USERNAME:

PASSWORD:

NOTES (EMAIL USED, ETC):

WEBSITE NAME:

WEBSITE ADDRESS:

USERNAME:

PASSWORD:

NOTES (EMAIL USED, ETC):

B

WEBSITE NAME:

WEBSITE ADDRESS:

USERNAME:

PASSWORD:

NOTES (EMAIL USED, ETC):

WEBSITE NAME:

WEBSITE ADDRESS:

USERNAME:

PASSWORD:

NOTES (EMAIL USED, ETC):

WEBSITE NAME:

WEBSITE ADDRESS:

USERNAME:

PASSWORD:

NOTES (EMAIL USED, ETC):

WEBSITE NAME:

WEBSITE ADDRESS:

USERNAME:

PASSWORD:

NOTES (EMAIL USED, ETC):

WEBSITE NAME:

WEBSITE ADDRESS:

USERNAME:

PASSWORD:

NOTES (EMAIL USED, ETC):

WEBSITE NAME:

WEBSITE ADDRESS:

USERNAME:

PASSWORD:

NOTES (EMAIL USED, ETC):

B

B

WEBSITE NAME:

WEBSITE ADDRESS:

USERNAME:

PASSWORD:

NOTES (EMAIL USED, ETC):

WEBSITE NAME:

WEBSITE ADDRESS:

USERNAME:

PASSWORD:

NOTES (EMAIL USED, ETC):

WEBSITE NAME:

WEBSITE ADDRESS:

USERNAME:

PASSWORD:

NOTES (EMAIL USED, ETC):

WEBSITE NAME:

WEBSITE ADDRESS:

USERNAME:

PASSWORD:

NOTES (EMAIL USED, ETC):

WEBSITE NAME:

WEBSITE ADDRESS:

USERNAME:

PASSWORD:

NOTES (EMAIL USED, ETC):

WEBSITE NAME:

WEBSITE ADDRESS:

USERNAME:

PASSWORD:

NOTES (EMAIL USED, ETC):

C

WEBSITE NAME:

WEBSITE ADDRESS:

USERNAME:

PASSWORD:

NOTES (EMAIL USED, ETC):

WEBSITE NAME:

WEBSITE ADDRESS:

USERNAME:

PASSWORD:

NOTES (EMAIL USED, ETC):

WEBSITE NAME:

WEBSITE ADDRESS:

USERNAME:

PASSWORD:

NOTES (EMAIL USED, ETC):

WEBSITE NAME:

WEBSITE ADDRESS:

USERNAME:

PASSWORD:

NOTES (EMAIL USED, ETC):

WEBSITE NAME:

WEBSITE ADDRESS:

USERNAME:

PASSWORD:

NOTES (EMAIL USED, ETC):

WEBSITE NAME:

WEBSITE ADDRESS:

USERNAME:

PASSWORD:

NOTES (EMAIL USED, ETC):

WEBSITE NAME:

WEBSITE ADDRESS:

USERNAME:

PASSWORD:

NOTES (EMAIL USED, ETC):

WEBSITE NAME:

WEBSITE ADDRESS:

USERNAME:

PASSWORD:

NOTES (EMAIL USED, ETC):

WEBSITE NAME:

WEBSITE ADDRESS:

USERNAME:

PASSWORD:

NOTES (EMAIL USED, ETC):

WEBSITE NAME:

WEBSITE ADDRESS:

USERNAME:

PASSWORD:

NOTES (EMAIL USED, ETC):

D

WEBSITE NAME:

WEBSITE ADDRESS:

USERNAME:

PASSWORD:

NOTES (EMAIL USED, ETC):

WEBSITE NAME:

WEBSITE ADDRESS:

USERNAME:

PASSWORD:

NOTES (EMAIL USED, ETC):

D

WEBSITE NAME:

WEBSITE ADDRESS:

USERNAME:

PASSWORD:

NOTES (EMAIL USED, ETC):

WEBSITE NAME:

WEBSITE ADDRESS:

USERNAME:

PASSWORD:

NOTES (EMAIL USED, ETC):

WEBSITE NAME:

WEBSITE ADDRESS:

USERNAME:

PASSWORD:

NOTES (EMAIL USED, ETC):

WEBSITE NAME:

WEBSITE ADDRESS:

USERNAME:

PASSWORD:

NOTES (EMAIL USED, ETC):

D

WEBSITE NAME:

WEBSITE ADDRESS:

USERNAME:

PASSWORD:

NOTES (EMAIL USED, ETC):

WEBSITE NAME:

WEBSITE ADDRESS:

USERNAME:

PASSWORD:

NOTES (EMAIL USED, ETC):

D

WEBSITE NAME:

WEBSITE ADDRESS:

USERNAME:

PASSWORD:

NOTES (EMAIL USED, ETC):

WEBSITE NAME:

WEBSITE ADDRESS:

USERNAME:

PASSWORD:

NOTES (EMAIL USED, ETC):

WEBSITE NAME:

WEBSITE ADDRESS:

USERNAME:

PASSWORD:

NOTES (EMAIL USED, ETC):

WEBSITE NAME:

WEBSITE ADDRESS:

USERNAME:

PASSWORD:

E

NOTES (EMAIL USED, ETC):

WEBSITE NAME:

WEBSITE ADDRESS:

USERNAME:

PASSWORD:

NOTES (EMAIL USED, ETC):

WEBSITE NAME:

WEBSITE ADDRESS:

USERNAME:

PASSWORD:

NOTES (EMAIL USED, ETC):

WEBSITE NAME:

WEBSITE ADDRESS:

USERNAME:

E **PASSWORD:**

NOTES (EMAIL USED, ETC):

WEBSITE NAME:

WEBSITE ADDRESS:

USERNAME:

PASSWORD:

NOTES (EMAIL USED, ETC):

WEBSITE NAME:

WEBSITE ADDRESS:

USERNAME:

PASSWORD:

NOTES (EMAIL USED, ETC):

WEBSITE NAME:

WEBSITE ADDRESS:

USERNAME:

PASSWORD:

E

NOTES (EMAIL USED, ETC):

WEBSITE NAME:

WEBSITE ADDRESS:

USERNAME:

PASSWORD:

NOTES (EMAIL USED, ETC):

WEBSITE NAME:

WEBSITE ADDRESS:

USERNAME:

PASSWORD:

NOTES (EMAIL USED, ETC):

WEBSITE NAME:

WEBSITE ADDRESS:

USERNAME:

E **PASSWORD:**

NOTES (EMAIL USED, ETC):

WEBSITE NAME:

WEBSITE ADDRESS:

USERNAME:

PASSWORD:

NOTES (EMAIL USED, ETC):

WEBSITE NAME:

WEBSITE ADDRESS:

USERNAME:

PASSWORD:

NOTES (EMAIL USED, ETC):

WEBSITE NAME:

WEBSITE ADDRESS:

USERNAME:

PASSWORD:

F

NOTES (EMAIL USED, ETC):

WEBSITE NAME:

WEBSITE ADDRESS:

USERNAME:

PASSWORD:

NOTES (EMAIL USED, ETC):

WEBSITE NAME:

WEBSITE ADDRESS:

USERNAME:

PASSWORD:

NOTES (EMAIL USED, ETC):

F

WEBSITE NAME:

WEBSITE ADDRESS:

USERNAME:

PASSWORD:

NOTES (EMAIL USED, ETC):

WEBSITE NAME:

WEBSITE ADDRESS:

USERNAME:

PASSWORD:

NOTES (EMAIL USED, ETC):

WEBSITE NAME:

WEBSITE ADDRESS:

USERNAME:

PASSWORD:

NOTES (EMAIL USED, ETC):

WEBSITE NAME:

WEBSITE ADDRESS:

USERNAME:

PASSWORD:

F

NOTES (EMAIL USED, ETC):

WEBSITE NAME:

WEBSITE ADDRESS:

USERNAME:

PASSWORD:

NOTES (EMAIL USED, ETC):

WEBSITE NAME:

WEBSITE ADDRESS:

USERNAME:

PASSWORD:

NOTES (EMAIL USED, ETC):

WEBSITE NAME:

WEBSITE ADDRESS:

USERNAME:

F PASSWORD:

NOTES (EMAIL USED, ETC):

WEBSITE NAME:

WEBSITE ADDRESS:

USERNAME:

PASSWORD:

NOTES (EMAIL USED, ETC):

WEBSITE NAME:

WEBSITE ADDRESS:

USERNAME:

PASSWORD:

NOTES (EMAIL USED, ETC):

WEBSITE NAME:

WEBSITE ADDRESS:

USERNAME:

PASSWORD:

NOTES (EMAIL USED, ETC):

WEBSITE NAME:

WEBSITE ADDRESS:

USERNAME:

PASSWORD:

NOTES (EMAIL USED, ETC):

WEBSITE NAME:

WEBSITE ADDRESS:

USERNAME:

PASSWORD:

NOTES (EMAIL USED, ETC):

WEBSITE NAME:

WEBSITE ADDRESS:

USERNAME:

PASSWORD:

G **NOTES (EMAIL USED, ETC):**

WEBSITE NAME:

WEBSITE ADDRESS:

USERNAME:

PASSWORD:

NOTES (EMAIL USED, ETC):

WEBSITE NAME:

WEBSITE ADDRESS:

USERNAME:

PASSWORD:

NOTES (EMAIL USED, ETC):

WEBSITE NAME:

WEBSITE ADDRESS:

USERNAME:

PASSWORD:

NOTES (EMAIL USED, ETC):

WEBSITE NAME:

WEBSITE ADDRESS:

USERNAME:

PASSWORD:

NOTES (EMAIL USED, ETC):

WEBSITE NAME:

WEBSITE ADDRESS:

USERNAME:

PASSWORD:

NOTES (EMAIL USED, ETC):

WEBSITE NAME:

WEBSITE ADDRESS:

USERNAME:

PASSWORD:

G NOTES (EMAIL USED, ETC):

WEBSITE NAME:

WEBSITE ADDRESS:

USERNAME:

PASSWORD:

NOTES (EMAIL USED, ETC):

WEBSITE NAME:

WEBSITE ADDRESS:

USERNAME:

PASSWORD:

NOTES (EMAIL USED, ETC):

WEBSITE NAME:

WEBSITE ADDRESS:

USERNAME:

PASSWORD:

NOTES (EMAIL USED, ETC):

H

WEBSITE NAME:

WEBSITE ADDRESS:

USERNAME:

PASSWORD:

NOTES (EMAIL USED, ETC):

WEBSITE NAME:

WEBSITE ADDRESS:

USERNAME:

PASSWORD:

NOTES (EMAIL USED, ETC):

WEBSITE NAME:

WEBSITE ADDRESS:

USERNAME:

PASSWORD:

NOTES (EMAIL USED, ETC):

H

WEBSITE NAME:

WEBSITE ADDRESS:

USERNAME:

PASSWORD:

NOTES (EMAIL USED, ETC):

WEBSITE NAME:

WEBSITE ADDRESS:

USERNAME:

PASSWORD:

NOTES (EMAIL USED, ETC):

WEBSITE NAME:

WEBSITE ADDRESS:

USERNAME:

PASSWORD:

NOTES (EMAIL USED, ETC):

H

WEBSITE NAME:

WEBSITE ADDRESS:

USERNAME:

PASSWORD:

NOTES (EMAIL USED, ETC):

WEBSITE NAME:

WEBSITE ADDRESS:

USERNAME:

PASSWORD:

NOTES (EMAIL USED, ETC):

WEBSITE NAME:

WEBSITE ADDRESS:

USERNAME:

PASSWORD:

NOTES (EMAIL USED, ETC):

H

WEBSITE NAME:

WEBSITE ADDRESS:

USERNAME:

PASSWORD:

NOTES (EMAIL USED, ETC):

WEBSITE NAME:

WEBSITE ADDRESS:

USERNAME:

PASSWORD:

NOTES (EMAIL USED, ETC):

WEBSITE NAME:

WEBSITE ADDRESS:

USERNAME:

PASSWORD:

NOTES (EMAIL USED, ETC):

I

WEBSITE NAME:

WEBSITE ADDRESS:

USERNAME:

PASSWORD:

NOTES (EMAIL USED, ETC):

WEBSITE NAME:

WEBSITE ADDRESS:

USERNAME:

PASSWORD:

NOTES (EMAIL USED, ETC):

WEBSITE NAME:

WEBSITE ADDRESS:

USERNAME:

PASSWORD:

NOTES (EMAIL USED, ETC):

I

WEBSITE NAME:

WEBSITE ADDRESS:

USERNAME:

PASSWORD:

NOTES (EMAIL USED, ETC):

WEBSITE NAME:

WEBSITE ADDRESS:

USERNAME:

PASSWORD:

NOTES (EMAIL USED, ETC):

WEBSITE NAME:

WEBSITE ADDRESS:

USERNAME:

PASSWORD:

NOTES (EMAIL USED, ETC):

WEBSITE NAME:

WEBSITE ADDRESS:

USERNAME:

PASSWORD:

NOTES (EMAIL USED, ETC):

WEBSITE NAME:

WEBSITE ADDRESS:

USERNAME:

PASSWORD:

NOTES (EMAIL USED, ETC):

WEBSITE NAME:

WEBSITE ADDRESS:

USERNAME:

PASSWORD:

NOTES (EMAIL USED, ETC):

I

WEBSITE NAME:

WEBSITE ADDRESS:

USERNAME:

PASSWORD:

NOTES (EMAIL USED, ETC):

WEBSITE NAME:

WEBSITE ADDRESS:

USERNAME:

PASSWORD:

NOTES (EMAIL USED, ETC):

WEBSITE NAME:

WEBSITE ADDRESS:

USERNAME:

PASSWORD:

NOTES (EMAIL USED, ETC):

WEBSITE NAME:

WEBSITE ADDRESS:

USERNAME:

PASSWORD:

NOTES (EMAIL USED, ETC):

WEBSITE NAME:

WEBSITE ADDRESS:

USERNAME:

PASSWORD:

NOTES (EMAIL USED, ETC):

WEBSITE NAME:

WEBSITE ADDRESS:

USERNAME:

PASSWORD:

NOTES (EMAIL USED, ETC):

J

WEBSITE NAME:

WEBSITE ADDRESS:

USERNAME:

PASSWORD:

NOTES (EMAIL USED, ETC):

WEBSITE NAME:

WEBSITE ADDRESS:

USERNAME:

PASSWORD:

NOTES (EMAIL USED, ETC):

WEBSITE NAME:

WEBSITE ADDRESS:

USERNAME:

PASSWORD:

NOTES (EMAIL USED, ETC):

WEBSITE NAME:

WEBSITE ADDRESS:

USERNAME:

PASSWORD:

NOTES (EMAIL USED, ETC):

WEBSITE NAME:

WEBSITE ADDRESS:

USERNAME:

PASSWORD:

NOTES (EMAIL USED, ETC):

WEBSITE NAME:

WEBSITE ADDRESS:

USERNAME:

PASSWORD:

NOTES (EMAIL USED, ETC):

J

WEBSITE NAME:

WEBSITE ADDRESS:

USERNAME:

PASSWORD:

NOTES (EMAIL USED, ETC):

WEBSITE NAME:

WEBSITE ADDRESS:

USERNAME:

PASSWORD:

NOTES (EMAIL USED, ETC):

WEBSITE NAME:

WEBSITE ADDRESS:

USERNAME:

PASSWORD:

NOTES (EMAIL USED, ETC):

WEBSITE NAME:

WEBSITE ADDRESS:

USERNAME:

PASSWORD:

NOTES (EMAIL USED, ETC):

WEBSITE NAME:

WEBSITE ADDRESS:

USERNAME:

PASSWORD:

NOTES (EMAIL USED, ETC):

WEBSITE NAME:

WEBSITE ADDRESS:

USERNAME:

PASSWORD:

NOTES (EMAIL USED, ETC):

J

WEBSITE NAME:

WEBSITE ADDRESS:

USERNAME:

PASSWORD:

NOTES (EMAIL USED, ETC):

WEBSITE NAME:

WEBSITE ADDRESS:

USERNAME:

PASSWORD:

NOTES (EMAIL USED, ETC):

WEBSITE NAME:

WEBSITE ADDRESS:

USERNAME:

PASSWORD:

NOTES (EMAIL USED, ETC):

WEBSITE NAME:

K

WEBSITE ADDRESS:

USERNAME:

PASSWORD:

NOTES (EMAIL USED, ETC):

WEBSITE NAME:

WEBSITE ADDRESS:

USERNAME:

PASSWORD:

NOTES (EMAIL USED, ETC):

WEBSITE NAME:

WEBSITE ADDRESS:

USERNAME:

PASSWORD:

NOTES (EMAIL USED, ETC):

K

WEBSITE NAME:

WEBSITE ADDRESS:

USERNAME:

PASSWORD:

NOTES (EMAIL USED, ETC):

WEBSITE NAME:

WEBSITE ADDRESS:

USERNAME:

PASSWORD:

NOTES (EMAIL USED, ETC):

WEBSITE NAME:

WEBSITE ADDRESS:

USERNAME:

PASSWORD:

NOTES (EMAIL USED, ETC):

WEBSITE NAME:

WEBSITE ADDRESS:

USERNAME:

PASSWORD:

NOTES (EMAIL USED, ETC):

WEBSITE NAME:

WEBSITE ADDRESS:

USERNAME:

PASSWORD:

NOTES (EMAIL USED, ETC):

WEBSITE NAME:

WEBSITE ADDRESS:

USERNAME:

PASSWORD:

NOTES (EMAIL USED, ETC):

K

WEBSITE NAME:

WEBSITE ADDRESS:

USERNAME:

PASSWORD:

NOTES (EMAIL USED, ETC):

WEBSITE NAME:

WEBSITE ADDRESS:

USERNAME:

PASSWORD:

NOTES (EMAIL USED, ETC):

WEBSITE NAME:

WEBSITE ADDRESS:

USERNAME:

PASSWORD:

NOTES (EMAIL USED, ETC):

WEBSITE NAME:

WEBSITE ADDRESS:

L

USERNAME:

PASSWORD:

NOTES (EMAIL USED, ETC):

WEBSITE NAME:

WEBSITE ADDRESS:

USERNAME:

PASSWORD:

NOTES (EMAIL USED, ETC):

WEBSITE NAME:

WEBSITE ADDRESS:

USERNAME:

PASSWORD:

NOTES (EMAIL USED, ETC):

WEBSITE NAME:

WEBSITE ADDRESS:

L

USERNAME:

PASSWORD:

NOTES (EMAIL USED, ETC):

WEBSITE NAME:

WEBSITE ADDRESS:

USERNAME:

PASSWORD:

NOTES (EMAIL USED, ETC):

WEBSITE NAME:

WEBSITE ADDRESS:

USERNAME:

PASSWORD:

NOTES (EMAIL USED, ETC):

WEBSITE NAME:

WEBSITE ADDRESS:

USERNAME:

PASSWORD:

NOTES (EMAIL USED, ETC):

L

WEBSITE NAME:

WEBSITE ADDRESS:

USERNAME:

PASSWORD:

NOTES (EMAIL USED, ETC):

WEBSITE NAME:

WEBSITE ADDRESS:

USERNAME:

PASSWORD:

NOTES (EMAIL USED, ETC):

WEBSITE NAME:

WEBSITE ADDRESS:

USERNAME:

PASSWORD:

NOTES (EMAIL USED, ETC):

L

WEBSITE NAME:

WEBSITE ADDRESS:

USERNAME:

PASSWORD:

NOTES (EMAIL USED, ETC):

WEBSITE NAME:

WEBSITE ADDRESS:

USERNAME:

PASSWORD:

NOTES (EMAIL USED, ETC):

WEBSITE NAME:

WEBSITE ADDRESS:

USERNAME:

PASSWORD:

NOTES (EMAIL USED, ETC):

M

WEBSITE NAME:

WEBSITE ADDRESS:

USERNAME:

PASSWORD:

NOTES (EMAIL USED, ETC):

WEBSITE NAME:

WEBSITE ADDRESS:

USERNAME:

PASSWORD:

NOTES (EMAIL USED, ETC):

WEBSITE NAME:

WEBSITE ADDRESS:

M **USERNAME:**

PASSWORD:

NOTES (EMAIL USED, ETC):

WEBSITE NAME:

WEBSITE ADDRESS:

USERNAME:

PASSWORD:

NOTES (EMAIL USED, ETC):

WEBSITE NAME:

WEBSITE ADDRESS:

USERNAME:

PASSWORD:

NOTES (EMAIL USED, ETC):

WEBSITE NAME:

WEBSITE ADDRESS:

USERNAME:

M

PASSWORD:

NOTES (EMAIL USED, ETC):

WEBSITE NAME:

WEBSITE ADDRESS:

USERNAME:

PASSWORD:

NOTES (EMAIL USED, ETC):

WEBSITE NAME:

WEBSITE ADDRESS:

USERNAME:

PASSWORD:

NOTES (EMAIL USED, ETC):

WEBSITE NAME:

WEBSITE ADDRESS:

M **USERNAME:**

PASSWORD:

NOTES (EMAIL USED, ETC):

WEBSITE NAME:

WEBSITE ADDRESS:

USERNAME:

PASSWORD:

NOTES (EMAIL USED, ETC):

WEBSITE NAME:

WEBSITE ADDRESS:

USERNAME:

PASSWORD:

NOTES (EMAIL USED, ETC):

WEBSITE NAME:

WEBSITE ADDRESS:

USERNAME:

PASSWORD:

N

NOTES (EMAIL USED, ETC):

WEBSITE NAME:

WEBSITE ADDRESS:

USERNAME:

PASSWORD:

NOTES (EMAIL USED, ETC):

WEBSITE NAME:

WEBSITE ADDRESS:

USERNAME:

PASSWORD:

NOTES (EMAIL USED, ETC):

WEBSITE NAME:

WEBSITE ADDRESS:

USERNAME:

N **PASSWORD:**

NOTES (EMAIL USED, ETC):

WEBSITE NAME:

WEBSITE ADDRESS:

USERNAME:

PASSWORD:

NOTES (EMAIL USED, ETC):

WEBSITE NAME:

WEBSITE ADDRESS:

USERNAME:

PASSWORD:

NOTES (EMAIL USED, ETC):

WEBSITE NAME:

WEBSITE ADDRESS:

USERNAME:

PASSWORD:

N

NOTES (EMAIL USED, ETC):

WEBSITE NAME:

WEBSITE ADDRESS:

USERNAME:

PASSWORD:

NOTES (EMAIL USED, ETC):

WEBSITE NAME:

WEBSITE ADDRESS:

USERNAME:

PASSWORD:

NOTES (EMAIL USED, ETC):

WEBSITE NAME:

WEBSITE ADDRESS:

USERNAME:

N **PASSWORD:**

NOTES (EMAIL USED, ETC):

WEBSITE NAME:

WEBSITE ADDRESS:

USERNAME:

PASSWORD:

NOTES (EMAIL USED, ETC):

WEBSITE NAME:

WEBSITE ADDRESS:

USERNAME:

PASSWORD:

NOTES (EMAIL USED, ETC):

WEBSITE NAME:

WEBSITE ADDRESS:

USERNAME:

PASSWORD:

NOTES (EMAIL USED, ETC):

O

WEBSITE NAME:

WEBSITE ADDRESS:

USERNAME:

PASSWORD:

NOTES (EMAIL USED, ETC):

WEBSITE NAME:

WEBSITE ADDRESS:

USERNAME:

PASSWORD:

NOTES (EMAIL USED, ETC):

WEBSITE NAME:

WEBSITE ADDRESS:

USERNAME:

PASSWORD:

0 **NOTES (EMAIL USED, ETC):**

WEBSITE NAME:

WEBSITE ADDRESS:

USERNAME:

PASSWORD:

NOTES (EMAIL USED, ETC):

WEBSITE NAME:

WEBSITE ADDRESS:

USERNAME:

PASSWORD:

NOTES (EMAIL USED, ETC):

WEBSITE NAME:

WEBSITE ADDRESS:

USERNAME:

PASSWORD:

NOTES (EMAIL USED, ETC):

O

WEBSITE NAME:

WEBSITE ADDRESS:

USERNAME:

PASSWORD:

NOTES (EMAIL USED, ETC):

WEBSITE NAME:

WEBSITE ADDRESS:

USERNAME:

PASSWORD:

NOTES (EMAIL USED, ETC):

WEBSITE NAME:

WEBSITE ADDRESS:

USERNAME:

PASSWORD:

O **NOTES (EMAIL USED, ETC):**

WEBSITE NAME:

WEBSITE ADDRESS:

USERNAME:

PASSWORD:

NOTES (EMAIL USED, ETC):

WEBSITE NAME:

WEBSITE ADDRESS:

USERNAME:

PASSWORD:

NOTES (EMAIL USED, ETC):

WEBSITE NAME:

WEBSITE ADDRESS:

USERNAME:

PASSWORD:

NOTES (EMAIL USED, ETC):

P

WEBSITE NAME:

WEBSITE ADDRESS:

USERNAME:

PASSWORD:

NOTES (EMAIL USED, ETC):

WEBSITE NAME:

WEBSITE ADDRESS:

USERNAME:

PASSWORD:

NOTES (EMAIL USED, ETC):

WEBSITE NAME:

WEBSITE ADDRESS:

USERNAME:

PASSWORD:

NOTES (EMAIL USED, ETC):

P

WEBSITE NAME:

WEBSITE ADDRESS:

USERNAME:

PASSWORD:

NOTES (EMAIL USED, ETC):

WEBSITE NAME:

WEBSITE ADDRESS:

USERNAME:

PASSWORD:

NOTES (EMAIL USED, ETC):

WEBSITE NAME:

WEBSITE ADDRESS:

USERNAME:

PASSWORD:

NOTES (EMAIL USED, ETC):

P

WEBSITE NAME:

WEBSITE ADDRESS:

USERNAME:

PASSWORD:

NOTES (EMAIL USED, ETC):

WEBSITE NAME:

WEBSITE ADDRESS:

USERNAME:

PASSWORD:

NOTES (EMAIL USED, ETC):

WEBSITE NAME:

WEBSITE ADDRESS:

USERNAME:

PASSWORD:

NOTES (EMAIL USED, ETC):

P

WEBSITE NAME:

WEBSITE ADDRESS:

USERNAME:

PASSWORD:

NOTES (EMAIL USED, ETC):

WEBSITE NAME:

WEBSITE ADDRESS:

USERNAME:

PASSWORD:

NOTES (EMAIL USED, ETC):

WEBSITE NAME:

WEBSITE ADDRESS:

USERNAME:

PASSWORD:

NOTES (EMAIL USED, ETC):

Q

WEBSITE NAME:

WEBSITE ADDRESS:

USERNAME:

PASSWORD:

NOTES (EMAIL USED, ETC):

WEBSITE NAME:

WEBSITE ADDRESS:

USERNAME:

PASSWORD:

NOTES (EMAIL USED, ETC):

WEBSITE NAME:

WEBSITE ADDRESS:

USERNAME:

PASSWORD:

NOTES (EMAIL USED, ETC):

Q

WEBSITE NAME:

WEBSITE ADDRESS:

USERNAME:

PASSWORD:

NOTES (EMAIL USED, ETC):

WEBSITE NAME:

WEBSITE ADDRESS:

USERNAME:

PASSWORD:

NOTES (EMAIL USED, ETC):

WEBSITE NAME:

WEBSITE ADDRESS:

USERNAME:

PASSWORD:

NOTES (EMAIL USED, ETC):

Q

WEBSITE NAME:

WEBSITE ADDRESS:

USERNAME:

PASSWORD:

NOTES (EMAIL USED, ETC):

WEBSITE NAME:

WEBSITE ADDRESS:

USERNAME:

PASSWORD:

NOTES (EMAIL USED, ETC):

WEBSITE NAME:

WEBSITE ADDRESS:

USERNAME:

PASSWORD:

NOTES (EMAIL USED, ETC):

Q

WEBSITE NAME:

WEBSITE ADDRESS:

USERNAME:

PASSWORD:

NOTES (EMAIL USED, ETC):

WEBSITE NAME:

WEBSITE ADDRESS:

USERNAME:

PASSWORD:

NOTES (EMAIL USED, ETC):

WEBSITE NAME:

WEBSITE ADDRESS:

USERNAME:

PASSWORD:

NOTES (EMAIL USED, ETC):

R

WEBSITE NAME:

WEBSITE ADDRESS:

USERNAME:

PASSWORD:

NOTES (EMAIL USED, ETC):

WEBSITE NAME:

WEBSITE ADDRESS:

USERNAME:

PASSWORD:

NOTES (EMAIL USED, ETC):

WEBSITE NAME:

WEBSITE ADDRESS:

USERNAME:

PASSWORD:

NOTES (EMAIL USED, ETC):

R

WEBSITE NAME:

WEBSITE ADDRESS:

USERNAME:

PASSWORD:

NOTES (EMAIL USED, ETC):

WEBSITE NAME:

WEBSITE ADDRESS:

USERNAME:

PASSWORD:

NOTES (EMAIL USED, ETC):

WEBSITE NAME:

WEBSITE ADDRESS:

USERNAME:

PASSWORD:

NOTES (EMAIL USED, ETC):

R

WEBSITE NAME:

WEBSITE ADDRESS:

USERNAME:

PASSWORD:

NOTES (EMAIL USED, ETC):

WEBSITE NAME:

WEBSITE ADDRESS:

USERNAME:

PASSWORD:

NOTES (EMAIL USED, ETC):

WEBSITE NAME:

WEBSITE ADDRESS:

USERNAME:

PASSWORD:

NOTES (EMAIL USED, ETC):

R

WEBSITE NAME:

WEBSITE ADDRESS:

USERNAME:

PASSWORD:

NOTES (EMAIL USED, ETC):

WEBSITE NAME:

WEBSITE ADDRESS:

USERNAME:

PASSWORD:

NOTES (EMAIL USED, ETC):

WEBSITE NAME:

WEBSITE ADDRESS:

USERNAME:

PASSWORD:

NOTES (EMAIL USED, ETC):

WEBSITE NAME:

WEBSITE ADDRESS:

USERNAME:

PASSWORD:

NOTES (EMAIL USED, ETC):

S

WEBSITE NAME:

WEBSITE ADDRESS:

USERNAME:

PASSWORD:

NOTES (EMAIL USED, ETC):

WEBSITE NAME:

WEBSITE ADDRESS:

USERNAME:

PASSWORD:

NOTES (EMAIL USED, ETC):

S

WEBSITE NAME:

WEBSITE ADDRESS:

USERNAME:

PASSWORD:

NOTES (EMAIL USED, ETC):

WEBSITE NAME:

WEBSITE ADDRESS:

USERNAME:

PASSWORD:

NOTES (EMAIL USED, ETC):

WEBSITE NAME:

WEBSITE ADDRESS:

USERNAME:

PASSWORD:

NOTES (EMAIL USED, ETC):

WEBSITE NAME:

WEBSITE ADDRESS:

USERNAME:

PASSWORD:

NOTES (EMAIL USED, ETC):

S

WEBSITE NAME:

WEBSITE ADDRESS:

USERNAME:

PASSWORD:

NOTES (EMAIL USED, ETC):

WEBSITE NAME:

WEBSITE ADDRESS:

USERNAME:

PASSWORD:

NOTES (EMAIL USED, ETC):

S

WEBSITE NAME:

WEBSITE ADDRESS:

USERNAME:

PASSWORD:

NOTES (EMAIL USED, ETC):

WEBSITE NAME:

WEBSITE ADDRESS:

USERNAME:

PASSWORD:

NOTES (EMAIL USED, ETC):

WEBSITE NAME:

WEBSITE ADDRESS:

USERNAME:

PASSWORD:

NOTES (EMAIL USED, ETC):

WEBSITE NAME:

WEBSITE ADDRESS:

USERNAME:

PASSWORD:

NOTES (EMAIL USED, ETC):

T

WEBSITE NAME:

WEBSITE ADDRESS:

USERNAME:

PASSWORD:

NOTES (EMAIL USED, ETC):

WEBSITE NAME:

WEBSITE ADDRESS:

USERNAME:

PASSWORD:

NOTES (EMAIL USED, ETC):

WEBSITE NAME:

WEBSITE ADDRESS:

USERNAME:

PASSWORD:

NOTES (EMAIL USED, ETC):

T

WEBSITE NAME:

WEBSITE ADDRESS:

USERNAME:

PASSWORD:

NOTES (EMAIL USED, ETC):

WEBSITE NAME:

WEBSITE ADDRESS:

USERNAME:

PASSWORD:

NOTES (EMAIL USED, ETC):

WEBSITE NAME:

WEBSITE ADDRESS:

USERNAME:

PASSWORD:

NOTES (EMAIL USED, ETC):

T

WEBSITE NAME:

WEBSITE ADDRESS:

USERNAME:

PASSWORD:

NOTES (EMAIL USED, ETC):

WEBSITE NAME:

WEBSITE ADDRESS:

USERNAME:

PASSWORD:

NOTES (EMAIL USED, ETC):

WEBSITE NAME:

WEBSITE ADDRESS:

USERNAME:

PASSWORD:

NOTES (EMAIL USED, ETC):

T

WEBSITE NAME:

WEBSITE ADDRESS:

USERNAME:

PASSWORD:

NOTES (EMAIL USED, ETC):

WEBSITE NAME:

WEBSITE ADDRESS:

USERNAME:

PASSWORD:

NOTES (EMAIL USED, ETC):

WEBSITE NAME:

WEBSITE ADDRESS:

USERNAME:

PASSWORD:

NOTES (EMAIL USED, ETC):

U

WEBSITE NAME:

WEBSITE ADDRESS:

USERNAME:

PASSWORD:

NOTES (EMAIL USED, ETC):

WEBSITE NAME:

WEBSITE ADDRESS:

USERNAME:

PASSWORD:

NOTES (EMAIL USED, ETC):

WEBSITE NAME:

WEBSITE ADDRESS:

U **USERNAME:**

PASSWORD:

NOTES (EMAIL USED, ETC):

WEBSITE NAME:

WEBSITE ADDRESS:

USERNAME:

PASSWORD:

NOTES (EMAIL USED, ETC):

WEBSITE NAME:

WEBSITE ADDRESS:

USERNAME:

PASSWORD:

NOTES (EMAIL USED, ETC):

WEBSITE NAME:

WEBSITE ADDRESS:

USERNAME:

PASSWORD:

NOTES (EMAIL USED, ETC):

U

WEBSITE NAME:

WEBSITE ADDRESS:

USERNAME:

PASSWORD:

NOTES (EMAIL USED, ETC):

WEBSITE NAME:

WEBSITE ADDRESS:

USERNAME:

PASSWORD:

NOTES (EMAIL USED, ETC):

WEBSITE NAME:

WEBSITE ADDRESS:

U **USERNAME:**

PASSWORD:

NOTES (EMAIL USED, ETC):

WEBSITE NAME:

WEBSITE ADDRESS:

USERNAME:

PASSWORD:

NOTES (EMAIL USED, ETC):

WEBSITE NAME:

WEBSITE ADDRESS:

USERNAME:

PASSWORD:

NOTES (EMAIL USED, ETC):

WEBSITE NAME:

WEBSITE ADDRESS:

USERNAME:

PASSWORD:

NOTES (EMAIL USED, ETC):

V

WEBSITE NAME:

WEBSITE ADDRESS:

USERNAME:

PASSWORD:

NOTES (EMAIL USED, ETC):

WEBSITE NAME:

WEBSITE ADDRESS:

USERNAME:

PASSWORD:

NOTES (EMAIL USED, ETC):

WEBSITE NAME:

WEBSITE ADDRESS:

USERNAME:

V **PASSWORD:**

NOTES (EMAIL USED, ETC):

WEBSITE NAME:

WEBSITE ADDRESS:

USERNAME:

PASSWORD:

NOTES (EMAIL USED, ETC):

WEBSITE NAME:

WEBSITE ADDRESS:

USERNAME:

PASSWORD:

NOTES (EMAIL USED, ETC):

WEBSITE NAME:

WEBSITE ADDRESS:

USERNAME:

PASSWORD:

NOTES (EMAIL USED, ETC):

V

WEBSITE NAME:

WEBSITE ADDRESS:

USERNAME:

PASSWORD:

NOTES (EMAIL USED, ETC):

WEBSITE NAME:

WEBSITE ADDRESS:

USERNAME:

PASSWORD:

NOTES (EMAIL USED, ETC):

WEBSITE NAME:

WEBSITE ADDRESS:

USERNAME:

V **PASSWORD:**

NOTES (EMAIL USED, ETC):

WEBSITE NAME:

WEBSITE ADDRESS:

USERNAME:

PASSWORD:

NOTES (EMAIL USED, ETC):

WEBSITE NAME:

WEBSITE ADDRESS:

USERNAME:

PASSWORD:

NOTES (EMAIL USED, ETC):

WEBSITE NAME:

WEBSITE ADDRESS:

USERNAME:

PASSWORD:

NOTES (EMAIL USED, ETC):

W

WEBSITE NAME:

WEBSITE ADDRESS:

USERNAME:

PASSWORD:

NOTES (EMAIL USED, ETC):

WEBSITE NAME:

WEBSITE ADDRESS:

USERNAME:

PASSWORD:

NOTES (EMAIL USED, ETC):

WEBSITE NAME:

WEBSITE ADDRESS:

USERNAME:

PASSWORD:

W **NOTES (EMAIL USED, ETC):**

WEBSITE NAME:

WEBSITE ADDRESS:

USERNAME:

PASSWORD:

NOTES (EMAIL USED, ETC):

WEBSITE NAME:

WEBSITE ADDRESS:

USERNAME:

PASSWORD:

NOTES (EMAIL USED, ETC):

WEBSITE NAME:

WEBSITE ADDRESS:

USERNAME:

PASSWORD:

NOTES (EMAIL USED, ETC):

W

WEBSITE NAME:

WEBSITE ADDRESS:

USERNAME:

PASSWORD:

NOTES (EMAIL USED, ETC):

WEBSITE NAME:

WEBSITE ADDRESS:

USERNAME:

PASSWORD:

NOTES (EMAIL USED, ETC):

WEBSITE NAME:

WEBSITE ADDRESS:

USERNAME:

PASSWORD:

W NOTES (EMAIL USED, ETC):

WEBSITE NAME:

WEBSITE ADDRESS:

USERNAME:

PASSWORD:

NOTES (EMAIL USED, ETC):

WEBSITE NAME:

WEBSITE ADDRESS:

USERNAME:

PASSWORD:

NOTES (EMAIL USED, ETC):

WEBSITE NAME:

WEBSITE ADDRESS:

USERNAME:

PASSWORD:

NOTES (EMAIL USED, ETC):

X

WEBSITE NAME:

WEBSITE ADDRESS:

USERNAME:

PASSWORD:

NOTES (EMAIL USED, ETC):

WEBSITE NAME:

WEBSITE ADDRESS:

USERNAME:

PASSWORD:

NOTES (EMAIL USED, ETC):

WEBSITE NAME:

WEBSITE ADDRESS:

USERNAME:

PASSWORD:

NOTES (EMAIL USED, ETC):

X

WEBSITE NAME:

WEBSITE ADDRESS:

USERNAME:

PASSWORD:

NOTES (EMAIL USED, ETC):

WEBSITE NAME:

WEBSITE ADDRESS:

USERNAME:

PASSWORD:

NOTES (EMAIL USED, ETC):

WEBSITE NAME:

WEBSITE ADDRESS:

USERNAME:

PASSWORD:

NOTES (EMAIL USED, ETC):

X

WEBSITE NAME:

WEBSITE ADDRESS:

USERNAME:

PASSWORD:

NOTES (EMAIL USED, ETC):

WEBSITE NAME:

WEBSITE ADDRESS:

USERNAME:

PASSWORD:

NOTES (EMAIL USED, ETC):

WEBSITE NAME:

WEBSITE ADDRESS:

USERNAME:

PASSWORD:

NOTES (EMAIL USED, ETC):

X

WEBSITE NAME:

WEBSITE ADDRESS:

USERNAME:

PASSWORD:

NOTES (EMAIL USED, ETC):

WEBSITE NAME:

WEBSITE ADDRESS:

USERNAME:

PASSWORD:

NOTES (EMAIL USED, ETC):

WEBSITE NAME:

WEBSITE ADDRESS:

USERNAME:

PASSWORD:

NOTES (EMAIL USED, ETC):

Y

WEBSITE NAME:

WEBSITE ADDRESS:

USERNAME:

PASSWORD:

NOTES (EMAIL USED, ETC):

WEBSITE NAME:

WEBSITE ADDRESS:

USERNAME:

PASSWORD:

NOTES (EMAIL USED, ETC):

WEBSITE NAME:

WEBSITE ADDRESS:

USERNAME:

PASSWORD:

NOTES (EMAIL USED, ETC):

Y

WEBSITE NAME:

WEBSITE ADDRESS:

USERNAME:

PASSWORD:

NOTES (EMAIL USED, ETC):

WEBSITE NAME:

WEBSITE ADDRESS:

USERNAME:

PASSWORD:

NOTES (EMAIL USED, ETC):

WEBSITE NAME:

WEBSITE ADDRESS:

USERNAME:

PASSWORD:

NOTES (EMAIL USED, ETC):

Y

WEBSITE NAME:

WEBSITE ADDRESS:

USERNAME:

PASSWORD:

NOTES (EMAIL USED, ETC):

WEBSITE NAME:

WEBSITE ADDRESS:

USERNAME:

PASSWORD:

NOTES (EMAIL USED, ETC):

WEBSITE NAME:

WEBSITE ADDRESS:

USERNAME:

PASSWORD:

NOTES (EMAIL USED, ETC):

Y

WEBSITE NAME:

WEBSITE ADDRESS:

USERNAME:

PASSWORD:

NOTES (EMAIL USED, ETC):

WEBSITE NAME:

WEBSITE ADDRESS:

USERNAME:

PASSWORD:

NOTES (EMAIL USED, ETC):

WEBSITE NAME:

WEBSITE ADDRESS:

USERNAME:

PASSWORD:

NOTES (EMAIL USED, ETC):

Z

WEBSITE NAME:

WEBSITE ADDRESS:

USERNAME:

PASSWORD:

NOTES (EMAIL USED, ETC):

WEBSITE NAME:

WEBSITE ADDRESS:

USERNAME:

PASSWORD:

NOTES (EMAIL USED, ETC):

WEBSITE NAME:

WEBSITE ADDRESS:

USERNAME:

PASSWORD:

NOTES (EMAIL USED, ETC):

Z

WEBSITE NAME:

WEBSITE ADDRESS:

USERNAME:

PASSWORD:

NOTES (EMAIL USED, ETC):

WEBSITE NAME:

WEBSITE ADDRESS:

USERNAME:

PASSWORD:

NOTES (EMAIL USED, ETC):

WEBSITE NAME:

WEBSITE ADDRESS:

USERNAME:

PASSWORD:

NOTES (EMAIL USED, ETC):

Z

WEBSITE NAME:

WEBSITE ADDRESS:

USERNAME:

PASSWORD:

NOTES (EMAIL USED, ETC):

WEBSITE NAME:

WEBSITE ADDRESS:

USERNAME:

PASSWORD:

NOTES (EMAIL USED, ETC):

WEBSITE NAME:

WEBSITE ADDRESS:

USERNAME:

PASSWORD:

NOTES (EMAIL USED, ETC):

Z

INTERNET SERVICE INFORMATION

INTERNET SERVICE PROVIDER:

ACCOUNT NUMBER:

CUSTOMER SERVICE NUMBER:

TECH SUPPORT NUMBER:

ROUTER INFO.

ROUTER MODEL:

ROUTER SERIAL NUMBER:

ROUTER IP ADDRESS:

MAC ADDRESS:

USER ID:

PASSWORD:

PIN:

WIRELESS INFO.

WIRELESS NAME (SSID):

SECURITY TYPE:

CHANNEL:

NETWORK SECURITY KEY:

EMAIL INFORMATION

EMAIL ADDRESS:

MAIL SERVER:

INCOMING SERVER:

OUTGOING SERVER:

PASSWORD:

EMAIL ADDRESS:

MAIL SERVER:

INCOMING SERVER:

OUTGOING SERVER:

PASSWORD:

EMAIL ADDRESS:

MAIL SERVER:

INCOMING SERVER:

OUTGOING SERVER:

PASSWORD:

SOFTWARE PRODUCT INFORMATION

SOFTWARE:

DATE OF PURCHASE:

PRODUCT ID:

PRODUCT / ACTIVATION KEY:

SOFTWARE:

DATE OF PURCHASE:

PRODUCT ID:

PRODUCT / ACTIVATION KEY:

SOFTWARE:

DATE OF PURCHASE:

PRODUCT ID:

PRODUCT / ACTIVATION KEY:

NOTES:

NOTES:

NOTES:

NOTES:

NOTES:

NOTES:

NOTES:

NOTES:

www.ingramcontent.com/pod-product-compliance
Lightning Source LLC
LaVergne TN
LVHW051704050326
832903LV00032B/3994